THIS JOURNAL BELONGS TO

....

Finally, brothers and sisters,
whatever is true, whatever is noble,
whatever is right, whatever is pure,
whatever is lovely, whatever is admirable—
if anything is excellent or praiseworthy—
think about such things.

PHILIPPIANS 4:8 NIV

*[God] is able to do far more abundantly beyond all that
we ask or think, according to the power that works within us.*

EPHESIANS 3:20 NASB

Kayea

I wuv ity fore

Kayla

i-Ready

Username EN1613

It is necessary that we dream now and then.
No one ever achieved anything from the smallest
to the greatest unless the dream was dreamed first.

LAURA INGALLS WILDER

But those who hope in the Lord will renew their strength.
They will soar on wings like eagles; they will run
and not grow weary, they will walk and not be faint.

ISAIAH 40:31 NIV

God designed us to be tremendously productive
and "to mount up with wings like eagles,"
realistically dreaming of what He can do with our potential.

CAROL KENT

$$\begin{array}{r} \overset{5}{3}\overset{4}{8}7 \\ \times\ \ \ 6 \\ \hline 2{,}326 \end{array}$$

It was God who first set the stars in space; He is their Maker
and Master—they are all in His hands and subject to His will.
Such are His power and His majesty. Behold your God!

J. I. PACKER

*Take delight in the Lord, and he will give you your
heart's desires. Commit everything you do to the Lord.
Trust him, and he will help you.*

PSALM 37:4-5 NLT

rch
role

*Our fulfillment comes in knowing God's glory,
loving Him for it, and delighting in it.*

The Lord will work out his plans for my life—
for your faithful love, O Lord, endures forever.

PSALM 138:8 NLT

Allow your dreams a place in your prayers and plans. God-given dreams can help you move into the future He is preparing for you.

Your eyes saw my unformed body; all the days ordained for me
were written in your book before one of them came to be.

PSALM 139:16 NIV

Every one of us as human beings is known and loved
by the Creator apart from every other human on earth.

JAMES DOBSON

We have this hope as an anchor for the soul, firm and secure.

HEBREWS 6:19 NIV

Faith goes up the stairs that love has made
and looks out the window which hope has opened.

CHARLES SPURGEON

How precious it is, Lord, to realize that you are thinking about me
constantly! I can't even count how many times a day your thoughts turn
toward me. And when I waken in the morning, you are still thinking of me!

PSALM 139:17–18 TLB

If you are seeking after God, you may be sure of this:
God is seeking you much more. He is the Lover,
and you are His beloved. He has promised Himself to you.

JOHN OF THE CROSS

For I am persuaded that neither death nor life...
nor any other created thing, shall be able to separate us
from the love of God which is in Christ Jesus our Lord.

ROMANS 8:38-39 NKJV

The grace of God means: Here is the world. Beautiful and terrible things will happen. Don't be afraid. I am with you. Nothing can ever separate us. It's for you I created the universe. I love you.

FREDERICK BUECHNER

So God created man in His own image;
in the image of God He created him; male and female He created them.

GENESIS 1:27 NKJV

All that we have and are is one of the unique and never-to-be repeated ways God has chosen to express Himself in space and time.

BRENNAN MANNING

Don't just pretend to love others. Really love them.
Hate what is wrong. Hold tightly to what is good. Love each other
with genuine affection, and take delight in honoring each other.

ROMANS 12:9-10 NLT

In God's wisdom, He frequently chooses to meet our needs by showing His love toward us through the hands and hearts of others.

JACK HAYFORD

*Now may the God of hope fill you with all joy and peace in believing,
that you may abound in hope by the power of the Holy Spirit.*

ROMANS 15:13 NKJV

Because You live, O Christ,
the spirit bird of hope is freed for flying,
our cages of despair no longer keep us
closed and life-denying.

SHIRLEY ERENA MURRAY

Do not fear, little flock, for it is your
Father's good pleasure to give you the kingdom.

LUKE 12:32 NKJV

At the very heart of the universe is God's desire to give.

I will give you hidden treasures,
riches stored in secret places,
so that you may know that I am the Lord,
the God of Israel, who summons you by name.

ISAIAH 45:3 NIV

*Lift up your eyes. Your heavenly Father waits to bless you—
in inconceivable ways to make your life what you never dreamed it could be.*

ANNE ORTLUND

Rest in the Lord, and wait patiently for Him.

PSALM 37:7 NKJV

When God finds a soul that rests in Him and is not easily moved...
to this same soul He gives the joy of His presence.

CATHERINE OF GENOA

Let us draw near to God with a sincere heart in full assurance of faith.... Let us hold unswervingly to the hope we profess, for he who promised is faithful.

HEBREWS 10:22–23 NIV

I have sought Thy nearness;
With all my heart have I called Thee,
And going out to meet Thee
I found Thee coming toward me.

YEHUDA HALEVI

I pray that your love will overflow more and more, and that you will keep on growing in your knowledge and understanding.

PHILIPPIANS 1:9 NLT

....

....

....

....

....

....

....

....

....

....

....

....

....

....

....

....

....

....

....

....

....

Open your hearts to the love God instills.... God loves you tenderly.
What He gives you is not to be kept under lock and key, but to be shared.

MOTHER TERESA

The Lord is my shepherd, I lack nothing.

PSALM 23:1 NIV

God never abandons anyone on whom He has set His love;
nor does Christ, the good shepherd, ever lose track of His sheep.

J. I. PACKER

A bruised reed he will not break,
and a smoldering wick he will not snuff out.

ISAIAH 42:3 NIV

A gentle word, like summer rain,
May soothe some heart and banish pain.
What joy or sadness often springs
From just the simple little things!

WILLA HOEY

*For you know that it was not with perishable things such
as silver or gold that you were redeemed...but with the precious
blood of Christ, a lamb without blemish or defect.*

1 PETER 1:18–19 NIV

*You are in the Beloved...therefore infinitely dear
to the Father, unspeakably precious to Him.*

NORMAN F. DOWTY

Taste and see that the Lord is good;
blessed is the one who takes refuge in him.
Fear the Lord, you his holy people,
for those who fear him lack nothing.

PSALM 34:8-9 NIV

*All that is good, all that is true, all that is beautiful, all that is beneficent,
be it great or small, be it perfect or fragmentary, natural as well
as supernatural, moral as well as material, comes from God.*

JOHN HENRY NEWMAN

He has made everything beautiful in its time.

ECCLESIASTES 3:11 NIV

Hope, like the gleaming taper's light,
Adorns and cheers our way;
And still, as darker grows the night,
Emits a brighter ray.

OLIVER GOLDSMITH

Whom have I in heaven but You? And besides You,
I desire nothing on earth. My flesh and my heart may fail,
but God is the strength of my heart and my portion forever.

PSALM 73:25-26 NASB

When God has become...our refuge and our fortress,
then we can reach out to Him in the midst of a broken world
and feel at home while still on the way.

HENRI J. M. NOUWEN

Remember, Lord, your great mercy and love, for they are from of old.

PSALM 25:6 NIV

God cannot give us a happiness and peace apart from Himself,
because it is not there. There is no such thing.

C. S. LEWIS

The Lord is my light and my salvation—whom shall I fear?...
For in the day of trouble He will keep me safe in His dwelling;
He will hide me in the shelter of His tabernacle.

PSALM 27:1, 4 NIV

Leave behind your fear and dwell on the lovingkindness of God,
that you may recover by gazing on Him.

And now these three remain: faith, hope and love.
But the greatest of these is love.

1 CORINTHIANS 13:13 NIV

God gives us dreams so we'll long for His reality.

BETH MOORE

How great are Your works, Lord, how profound Your thoughts!

PSALM 92:5 NIV

Just when we least expect it, [God] intrudes into our
neat and tidy notions about who He is and how He works.

JONI EARECKSON TADA

*See what great love the Father has lavished on us,
that we should be called children of God! And that is what we are!*

1 JOHN 3:1 NIV

When we call on God, He bends down His ear to listen,
as a father bends down to listen to his little child.

ELIZABETH CHARLES

May all who love you be like the sun when it rises in its strength.

JUDGES 5:31 NIV

*See each morning a world made anew, as if it were
the morning of the very first day; treasure and use it,
as if it were the final hour of the very last day.*

FAY HARTZELL ARNOLD

They speak of the glorious splendor of your majesty—
and I will meditate on your wonderful works.

PSALM 145:5 NIV

Go outside, to the fields, enjoy nature and the sunshine,
go out and try to recapture happiness in yourself and in God.
Think of all the beauty that's still left in and around you and be happy!

ANNE FRANK

You are my hiding place and my shield;
I wait for Your word.

PSALM 119:114 NASB

*Be still, and in the quiet moments, listen to the voice
of your heavenly Father. His words can renew your spirit...
no one knows you and your needs like He does.*

JANET L. SMITH

Nevertheless, each person should live as a believer in whatever situation the Lord has assigned to them, just as God has called them.

1 CORINTHIANS 7:17 NIV

Use what talents you possess: the woods would be very silent
if no birds sang there except those that sang best.

HENRY VAN DYKE

You will keep in perfect peace those whose minds are steadfast,
because they trust in You. Trust in the Lord forever,
for the Lord, the Lord, is the Rock eternal.

ISAIAH 26:3-4 NIV

The God of peace gives perfect peace to those
whose hearts are stayed upon Him.

CHARLES SPURGEON

He will yet fill your mouth with laughter and your lips with shouts of joy.

JOB 8:21 NIV

*The laughter that springs from love makes wide
the space around it—gives room for the loved one to enter in.
Real laughter welcomes, and never shuts out.*

EUGENIA PRICE

*Ah Lord God! Behold, You have made the heavens
and the earth by Your great power and by Your outstretched arm!
Nothing is too difficult for You.*

JEREMIAH 32:17 NASB

Whatever the circumstances, whatever the call...
His strength will be your strength in your hour of need.

The joy of the Lord is your strength.

NEHEMIAH 8:10 NKJV

If one is joyful, it means that one is faithfully living for God,
and that nothing else counts; and if one gives joy to others
one is doing God's work. With joy without and joy within, all is well.

*All the days ordained for me were written
in Your book before one of them came to be.*

PSALM 139:16 NIV

*The patterns of our days are always rearranging...and each design
for living is unique, graced with its own special beauty.*

For with God all things are possible.

MARK 10:27 NKJV

Faith is not a sense, not sight, not reason, but a taking God at His Word.

EVANS

*The Lord will guide you always; he will satisfy your needs
in a sun-scorched land and will strengthen your frame. You will be like
a well-watered garden, like a spring whose waters never fail.*

ISAIAH 58:11 NIV

*It is God's knowledge of me, His careful husbanding
of the ground of my being, His constant presence
in the garden of my little life that guarantees my joy.*

W. PHILLIP KELLER

*It is good to give thanks to the Lord and to sing praises
to Your name, O Most High; to declare Your lovingkindness
in the morning and Your faithfulness by night.*

PSALM 92:1–2 NASB

*Morning has broken like the first morning, Blackbird has spoken
like the first bird.... Praise with elation, praise every morning,
God's re-creation of the new day!*

ELEANOR FARJEON

Whatever you do in word or deed, do all in the name of the Lord Jesus,
giving thanks to God the Father through Him.

COLOSSIANS 3:17 NKJV

Walk softly. Speak tenderly. Love fervently.

I have set the Lord always before me;
because He is at my right hand I shall not be moved.

PSALM 16:8 NKJV

God still draws near to us in the ordinary, commonplace,
everyday experiences and places.... He comes in surprising ways.

HENRY GARIEPY

Do not fear, for I have redeemed you;
I have summoned you by one; you are mine.

ISAIAH 43:1 NIV

Nothing we can do will make the Father love us less;
nothing we do can make Him love us more.
He loves us unconditionally with an everlasting love.

How lovely are Your dwelling places, O Lord of hosts!
My soul longed and even yearned for the courts of the Lord.

PSALM 84:1-2 NASB

We walk without fear, full of hope and courage
and strength to do His will, waiting for the endless good
which He is always giving as fast as He can get us able to take it in.

GEORGE MACDONALD

You have made known to me the paths of life;
You will fill me with joy in your presence.

ACTS 2:28 NIV

To wake each morn as if the Maker's grace
Did us afresh from nothingness derive,
That we might sing, "How happy is our case!
How beautiful it is to be alive."

HENRY SEPTIMUS SUTTON

Come, and let us go up to the mountain of the Lord....
He will teach us His ways, and we shall walk in His paths.

MICAH 4:2 NKJV

*The best things are nearest...light in your eyes, flowers at your feet,
duties at your hand, the path of God just before you.*

ROBERT LOUIS STEVENSON

Because of Christ and our faith in him,
we can now come boldly and confidently into God's presence.

EPHESIANS 3:12 NLT

*Great faith isn't the ability to believe long and far into the misty future.
It's simply taking God at His word and taking the next step.*

JONI EARECKSON TADA

A friend loves at all times.

PROVERBS 17:17 NKJV

Caring words, friendship, affectionate touch—all of these have a healing quality. Why? Because we were all created by God to give and receive love.

JACK FROST

For He will give His angels charge concerning you,
to guard you in all your ways.

PSALM 91:11 NASB

God takes care of His own. He knows our needs.
He anticipates our crises. He is moved by our weaknesses.
He stands ready to come to our rescue.

CHARLES R. SWINDOLL

You, Lord, are a compassionate and gracious God,
slow to anger, abounding in love and faithfulness.

PSALM 86:14–16 NIV

*The loving God we serve has immeasurable compassion
and tenderness toward each of us throughout our lives.*

JAMES DOBSON

I will bless the Lord at all times;
His praise shall continually be in my mouth.

PSALM 34:1 NKJV

*Our inner happiness depends not on what we experience
but on the degree of our gratitude to God, whatever the experience.*

ALBERT SCHWEITZER

I will give them an undivided heart and put a new spirit in them;
I will remove from them their heart of stone and give them
a heart of flesh. Then...they will be my people, and I will be their God.

EZEKIEL 11:19–20 NIV

*In the deepest heart of everyone, God planted
a longing for Himself as He is: a God of love.*

EUGENIA PRICE

*Also, he has put eternity into man's heart, yet so that he cannot
find out what God has done from the beginning to the end.*

ECCLESIASTES 3:11 ESV

*Our Creator would never have made such lovely days,
and given us the deep hearts to enjoy them, above and beyond
all thought, unless we were meant to be immortal.*

NATHANIEL HAWTHORNE

The heavens declare His righteousness, and all the peoples see His glory.

PSALM 97:6 NKJV

He made you so you could share in His creation,
could love and laugh and know Him.

TED GRIFFEN

Give us day by day our daily bread.

LUKE 11:3 NKJV

To be grateful is to recognize the Love of God in everything
He has given us—and He has given us everything.

— THOMAS MERTON

The thief comes only to steal and kill and destroy;
I have come that they may have life, and have it to the full.

JOHN 10:10 NIV

He is looking for people who will come in simple dependence upon His grace.... At this very moment, He's looking at you.

JACK HAYFORD

God has given each of you some special abilities; be sure to use them to help each other, passing on to others God's many kinds of blessings.

1 PETER 4:10 TLB

God has a wonderful plan for each person He has chosen.
He knew even before He created this world what beauty
He would bring forth from our lives.

LOUIS B. WYLY

But seek first his kingdom and his righteousness,
and all these things will be given to you as well.

MATTHEW 6:33 NIV

Trust the past to the mercy of God, the present to His love,
and the future to His providence.

AUGUSTINE

Finally, all of you, be like-minded, be sympathetic,
love one another, be compassionate and humble.

1 PETER 3:8 NIV

*When one has once fully entered the realm of love, the world—
no matter how imperfect—becomes rich and beautiful,
for it consists solely of opportunities for love.*

SOREN KIERKEGAARD

Every good gift and every perfect gift is from above, and comes down from the Father of lights, with whom is no variation or shadow of turning.

JAMES 1:17 NKJV

*All perfect gifts are from above and all our blessings show
The amplitude of God's dear love which any heart may know.*

LAURA LEE RANDALL

The Lord is good to them who wait for Him, to the soul that seeks Him.

LAMENTATIONS 3:25 NKJV

Unlovely myself, I rushed towards all those lovely things
You had made. And always You were with me.

AUGUSTINE

Thanks be to God for His indescribable gift!

Love is the response of the heart to the overwhelming
goodness of God. You may be so awestruck and full of love
at His presence that words do not come.

RICHARD J. FOSTER

I will lead the blind by ways they have not known,
along unfamiliar paths I will guide them;
I will turn the darkness into light before them
and make the rough places smooth.

ISAIAH 42:16 NIV

....
....
....
....
....
....
....
....
....
....
....
....
....
....
....
....
....
....
....
....
....

Heaven often seems distant and unknown, but if He who made the road...is our guide, we need not fear to lose the way.

HENRY VAN DYKE

The Lord will command His lovingkindness in the daytime;
and His song will be with me in the night, a prayer to the God of my life.

PSALM 42:8 NASB

Life is what we are alive to. It is not length but breadth.
Be alive to goodness, kindness, purity, love, history,
poetry, music, flowers, stars, God, and eternal hope.

MALTBI D. BABCOCK

Therefore, since we have been justified through faith,
we have peace with God through our Lord Jesus Christ.

ROMANS 5:1 NIV

Whoever walks toward God one step, God runs toward him two.

*You will make known to me the path of life; in Your presence
is fullness of joy; in Your right hand there are pleasures forever.*

Those who run in the path of God's commands have their hearts set free.

They do not say to themselves, "Let us fear the Lord our God,
who gives autumn and spring rain in season,
who assures us of the regular weeks of harvest."

JEREMIAH 5:24 NIV

....

....

....

....

....

....

....

....

....

....

....

....

....

....

....

....

....

....

....

....

....

....

....

....

....

....

....

....

....

....

....

....

....

....

....

....

In waiting we begin to get in touch with the rhythms of life—
stillness and action, listening and decision. They are the rhythms
of God. It is in the everyday and the commonplace that we learn
patience, acceptance, and contentment.

RICHARD J. FOSTER

*I am the vine; you are the branches. If you remain in me and I in you,
you will bear much fruit; apart from me you can do nothing.*

JOHN 15:5 NIV

This is and has been the Father's work from the beginning—
to bring us into the home of His heart.

GEORGE MACDONALD

Worship the Lord in the beauty of holiness.

PSALM 96:9 NKJV

All the world is an utterance of the Almighty. Its countless beauties,
its exquisite adaptations, all speak to you of Him.

PHILLIPS BROOKS

*I pray that out of his glorious riches he may strengthen you
with power through his Spirit in your inner being,
so that Christ may dwell in your hearts through faith.*

EPHESIANS 3:16-17 NIV

Lord, give me only Your love and Your grace.
With this I am rich enough, and I have no more to ask.

IGNATIUS OF LOYOLA

Oh sing to the Lord a new song! Sing to the Lord, all the earth.

PSALM 96:1 NKJV

God's quest to be glorified and our quest to be satisfied reach their goal in this one experience: our delight in God which overflows in praise.

JOHN PIPER

Be beautiful inside, in your hearts, with the lasting charm
of a gentle and quiet spirit which is so precious to God.

1 PETER 3:4 TLB

Give yourself to God and then be what and who you are without regard to what others think.... Learn to pray inwardly every moment.

A. W. TOZER

The Lord your God will change your heart and the hearts
of all your descendants, so that you will love him
with all your heart and soul and so you may live!

DEUTERONOMY 30:6 NLT

I asked God for all things that I might enjoy life.
He gave me life that I might enjoy all things.

One thing I have asked from the Lord, that I shall seek:
That I may dwell in the house of the Lord all the days of my life,
To behold the beauty of the Lord and to meditate in His temple.

PSALM 27:4 NASB

There are two kinds of people in the world: those who come into a room and say, "Here I am!" and those who come in and say, "Ah, there you are!"

Why spend money on what is not bread,
and your labor on what does not satisfy?
Listen, listen to me, and eat what is good,
and you will delight in the richest of fare.

ISAIAH 55:2 NIV

I will remember that when I give Him my heart,
God chooses to live within me—body and soul.
He fills all of the empty places, His very Spirit inside of me.

For now we see only a reflection as in a mirror; then we shall see face to face.
Now I know in part; then I shall know fully, even as I am fully known.

1 CORINTHIANS 13:12 NIV

*From the world we see, hear, and touch, we behold inspired visions
that reveal God's glory...May God give you eyes to see
beauty only the heart can understand.*

Come to me, all you who are weary and burdened,
and I will give you rest.

MATTHEW 11:28 NIV

It is the simple things of life that make living worthwhile,
the sweet fundamental things such as love and duty,
work and rest, and living close to nature.

LAURA INGALLS WILDER

And I pray that you, being rooted and established in love,
may have power, together with all the Lord's holy people,
to grasp how wide and long and high and deep is the love of Christ.

EPHESIANS 3:17–18 NIV

The wonder of living is held within the beauty of silence,
the glory of sunlight... the sweetness of fresh spring air, the quiet strength
of earth, and the love that lies at the very root of all things.

Ellie Claire® Gift & Paper Expressions
Franklin, TN 37067
EllieClaire.com
Ellie Claire is a registered trademark of Worthy Media, Inc.

Whatever Is Lovely Journal
© 2016 by Ellie Claire
Published by Ellie Claire, an imprint of Worthy Publishing Group,
a division of Worthy Media, Inc.

ISBN 978-1-63326-154-9

Stock or custom editions of Ellie Claire titles may be purchased in bulk for educational,
business, ministry, fundraising, or sales promotional use. For information, please e-mail
info@EllieClaire.com

Compiled by Jennifer Gerelds
Cover illustration by Lisa Glanz | CreativeMarket.com

Printed in China

4 5 6 7 8 9 10 11 12 RRD 23 22 21 20 19 18